Authentic

The Distance to Here

MW00560083

Live Website: www.friendsoflive.com   Live Info Hotline: (610) 866-8661
Fan Club Info - Send a #10 stamped envelope to:
Friends of Live
P.O.Box 20266
Lehigh Valley, PA 18002-0266

Photos by Danny Clinch

Transcribed by Steve Gorenberg, Bill LaFleur and Pete Sawchuck
Artwork © 1999 Radioactive Records
Special thanks to Julie Sauerzopf at Media Five Ltd.

Project Managers: Jeannette DeLisa and Aaron Stang
Book Art Layout: Joann Carrera

Contents

THE DOLPHIN'S CRY

Words and Music by
Edward Kowalczyk

All gtrs. tune down 1/2 step:

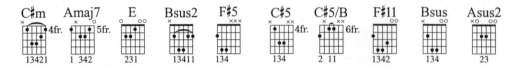

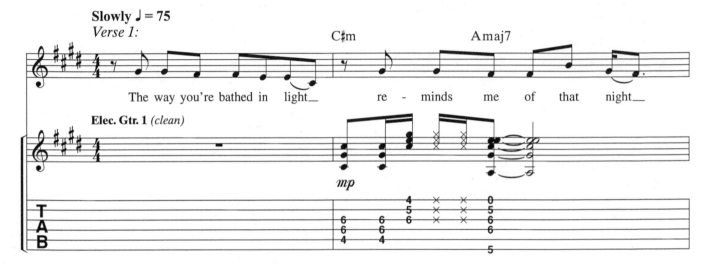

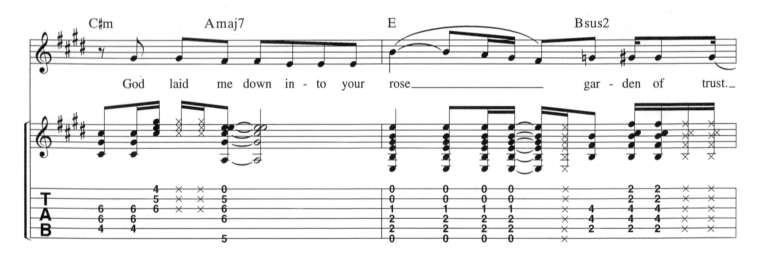

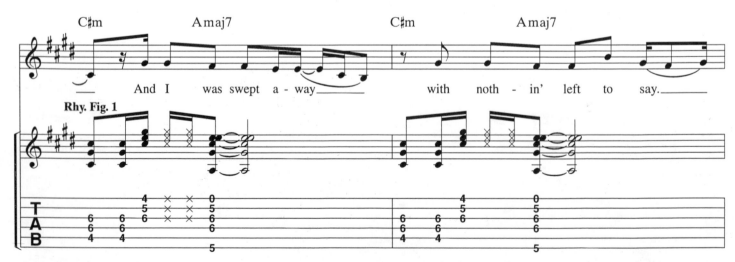

The Dolphin's Cry - 10 - 1
PG9911

*Set to produce pitches one octave above fretted notes.

The Dolphin's Cry - 10 - 2
PG9911

8

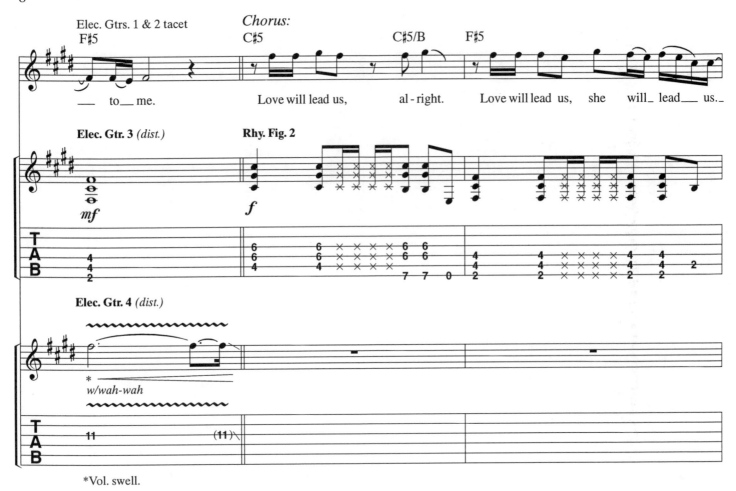

*Vol. swell.

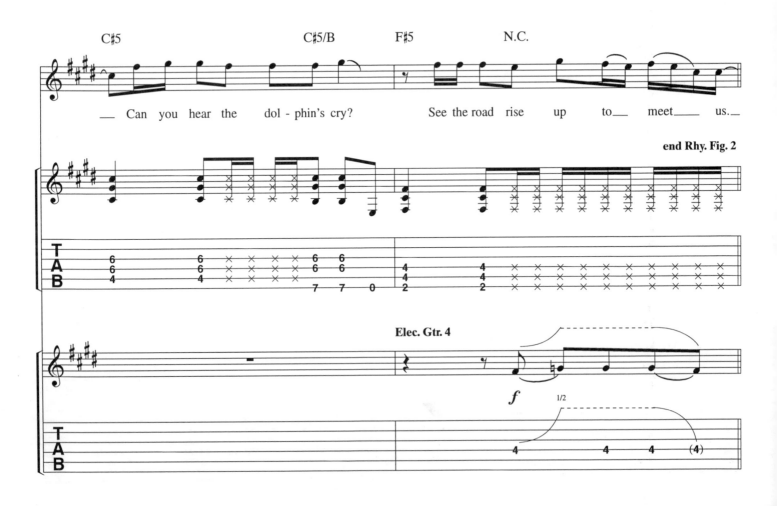

The Dolphin's Cry - 10 - 4
PG9911

10

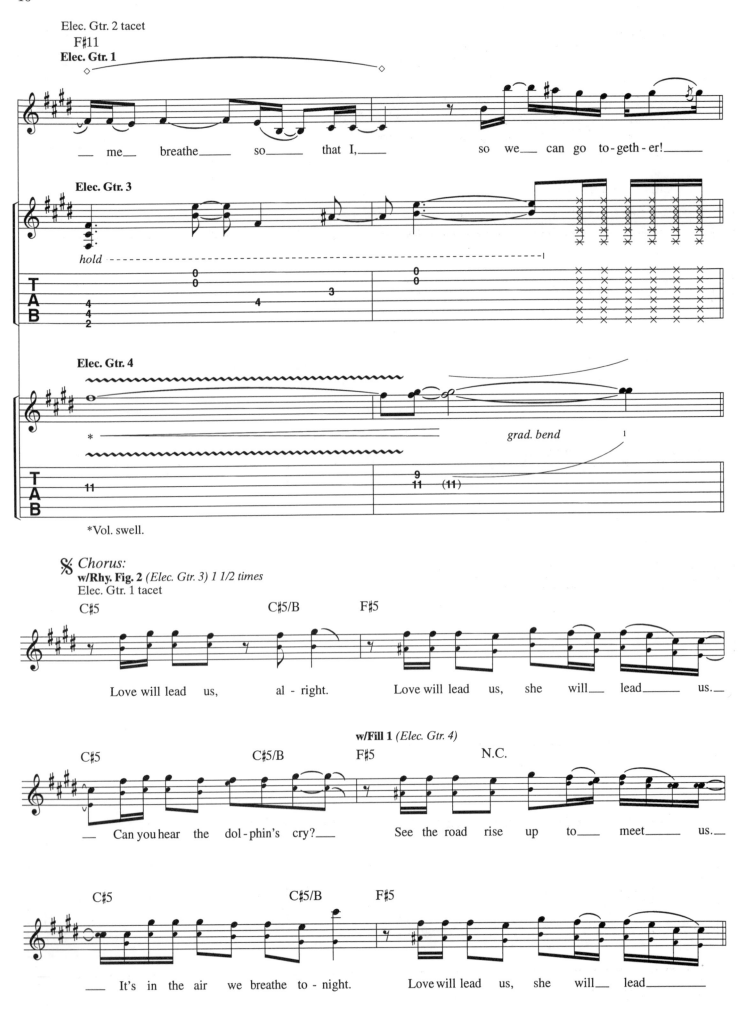

Bridge:
w/ Fill 2 *(Elec. Gtr. 5) 2nd time only*

us._____ Life is like__ a shoot - in' star.____ It don't mat - ter who_

___ you are__ if you on - ly run__ for cov - er.____ It's just a waste of time._

12

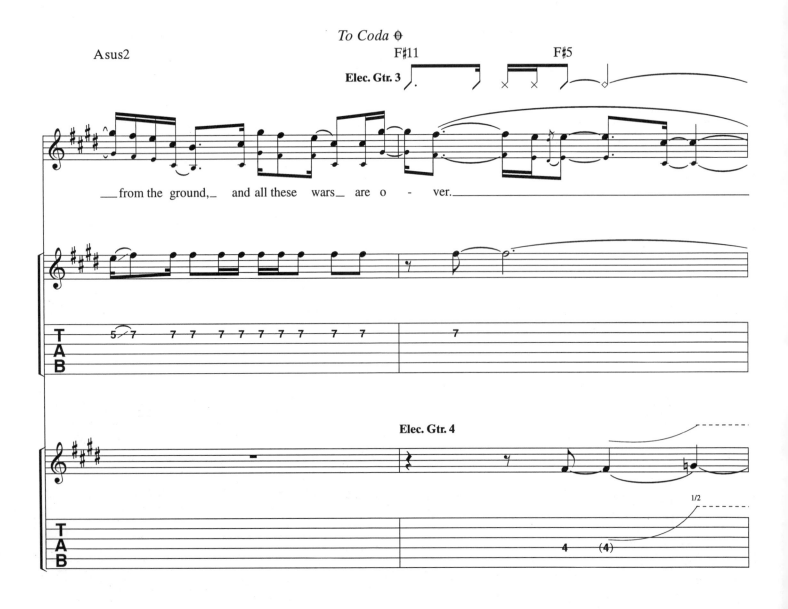

Interlude:
w/Rhy. Fig. 1 (Elec. Gtr. 1) 2 times
Elec. Gtrs. 3 & 5 tacet
C♯m Amaj7 C♯m Amaj7
O - ver. O -
Elec. Gtr. 2
8va
loco
A.H.
whammy pedal off
C♯m Amaj7 E Bsus2
ver. Sing-in', la, da, da, da, da, da, da. O -
C♯m Amaj7 C♯m Amaj7 C♯m Amaj7
- ver. (Whispered:) Come to me. Come to me. Yeah, la, da, da, da,
8va

14

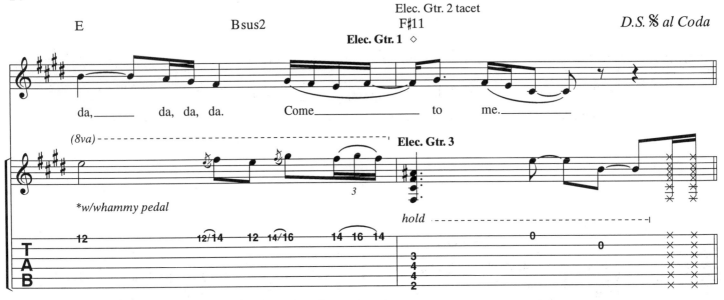

*Set to produce pitches one octave above fretted notes.

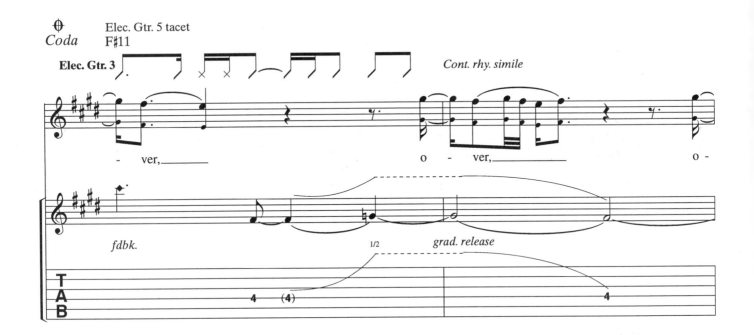

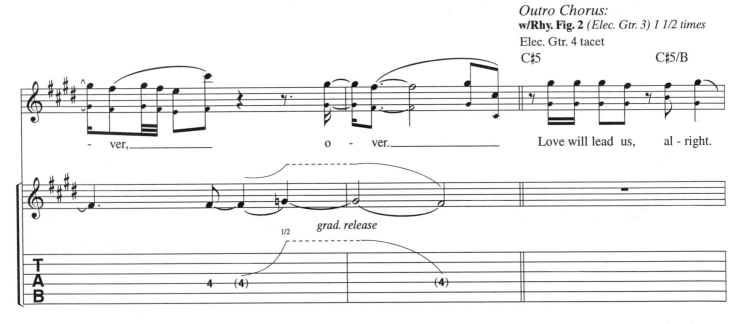

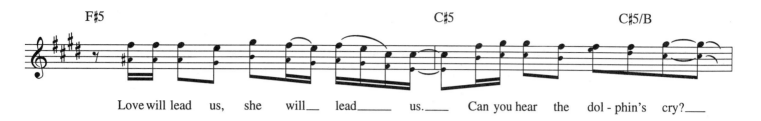

Love will lead us, she will lead us. Can you hear the dol-phin's cry?

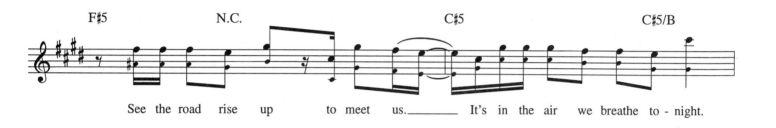

See the road rise up to meet us. It's in the air we breathe to-night.

Begin fade
w/Rhy. Fig. 2 *(Elec. Gtr. 3) 1 1/4 times*

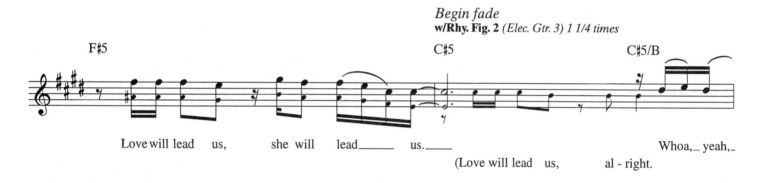

Love will lead us, she will lead us. Whoa, yeah,
(Love will lead us, al-right.

al - right. Al - right.
Do it o - ver, she will lead us. Love will lead us, al - right.

Fade

Al - right.
If you sur-ren-der, love will save us. Love will lead us, al - right.)

THE DISTANCE

Words and Music by
Edward Kowalczyk

Let him come in-to the cit - y. Let him find his luck-y pen-ny. Let him

put it in his pock-et and shake___ it all a-round.

*Doubled by Acous. Gtr. throughout.

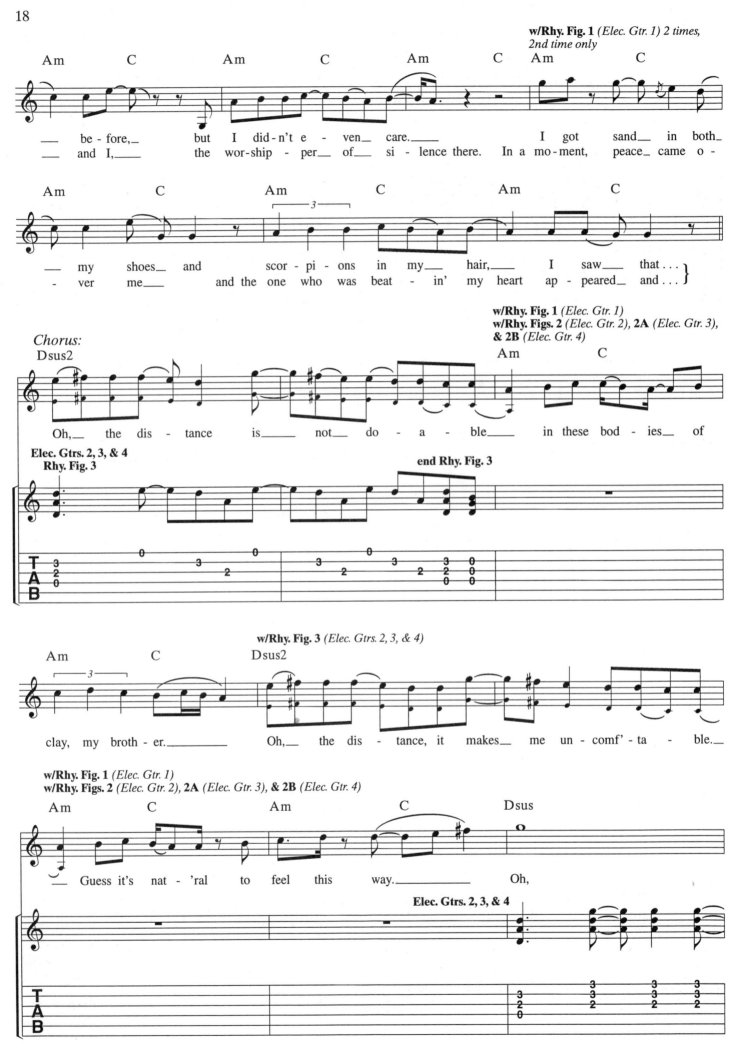

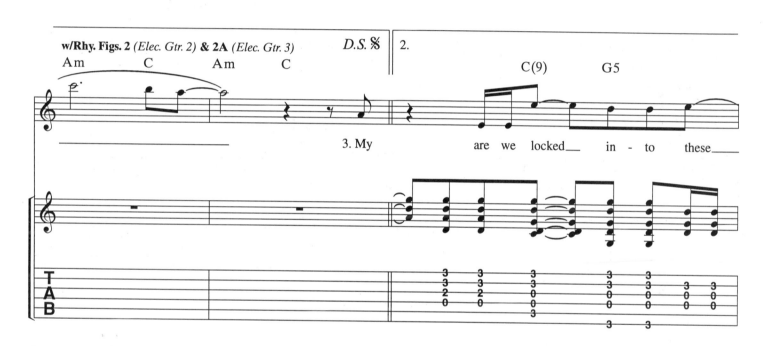

20

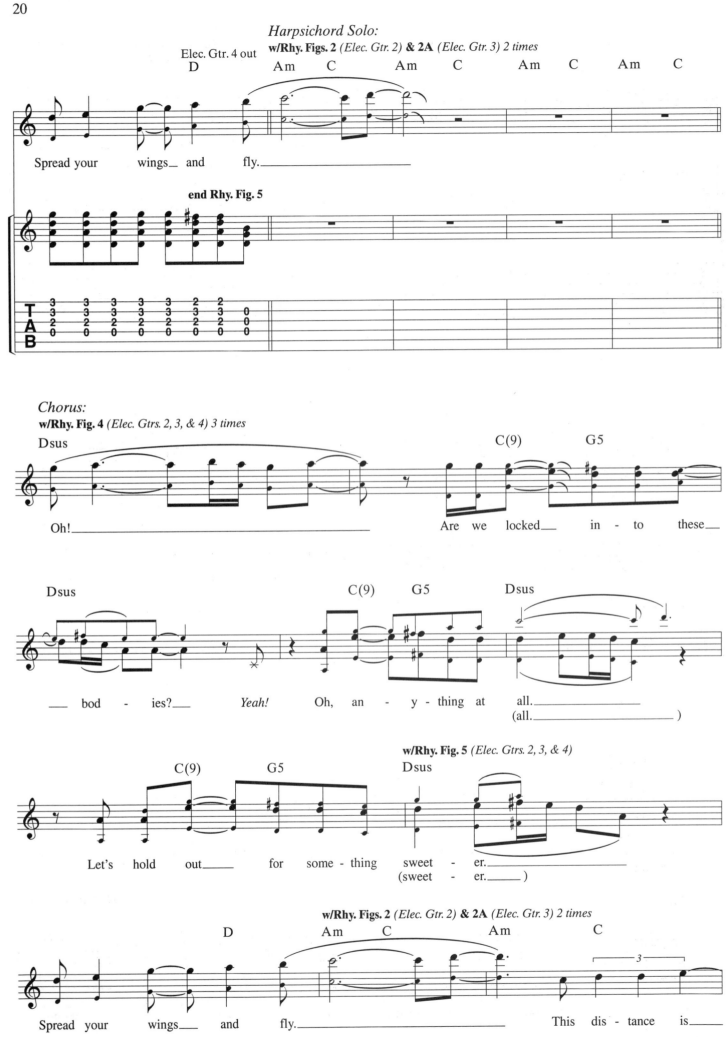

The Distance - 6 - 5
PG9911

Outro:
w/Rhy. Figs. 2 (Elec. Gtr. 2), **2A** (Elec. Gtr. 3),
& 2B (Elec. Gtr. 4) till fade

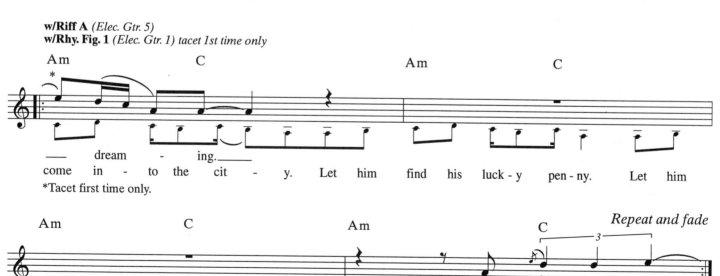

SPARKLE

Words and Music by
Edward Kowalczyk

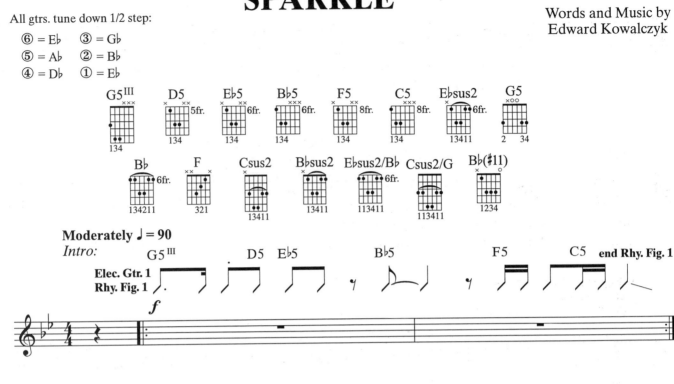

*Harmony implied by bass.
†Second time only.

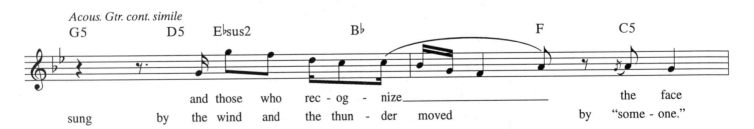

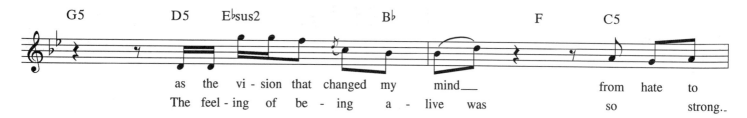

G5   D5   E♭sus2   B♭   F   C5

as the vi - sion that changed my mind___ from hate to
The feel - ing of be - ing a - live was so strong..

w/Fill 1 *(Elec. Gtr. 1)*

G5   D5   E♭sus2   B♭   F   C5

faith, was as sim - ple as grapes to wine_____ and sweet as_____
— The giv - er be - came the gift, all one.

w/Rhy. Fig. 1 *(Elec. Gtr. 1)* *4 times*
Acous. Gtr. out

G5 III   D5   E♭5   B♭5   F5   C5

— I'm gath - er - ing up___ my friends_____ to - day._____
The day that I was_____ so_____ sweet-ly___ sung.

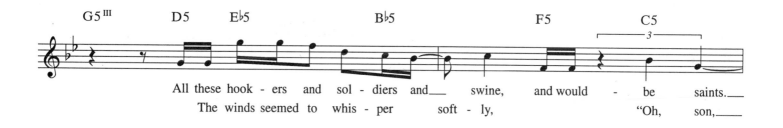

G5 III   D5   E♭5   B♭5   F5   C5

All these hook - ers and sol - diers and___ swine, and would - be saints.___
The winds seemed to whis - per soft - ly, "Oh, son,___

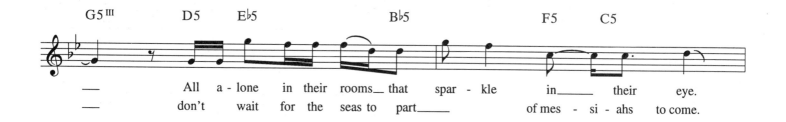

G5 III   D5   E♭5   B♭5   F5   C5

— All a - lone in their rooms___ that spar - kle in___ their eye.
— don't wait for the seas to part_____ of mes - si - ahs to come.

Fill 1
Elec. Gtr. 1

24

Play a song that they'll come out - side_____ to see if . . .
Don't sit a - round and waste this chance to see it!"

Chorus:

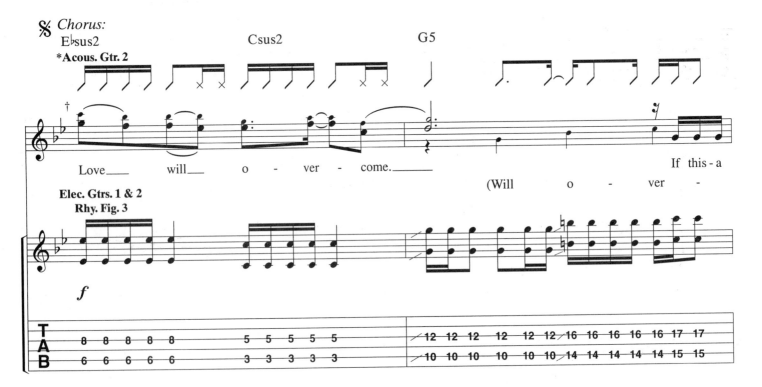

Love____ will____ o - ver - come.____ If this - a
(Will o - ver -

*Last time only.
†All backing vocals tacet first time only.

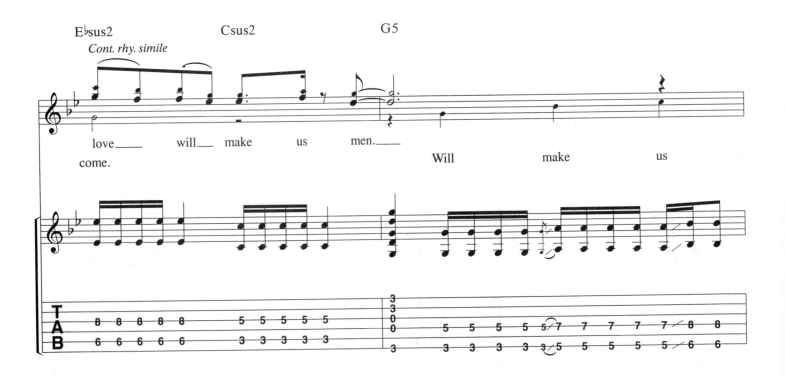

love____ will____ make us men.____
come. Will make us

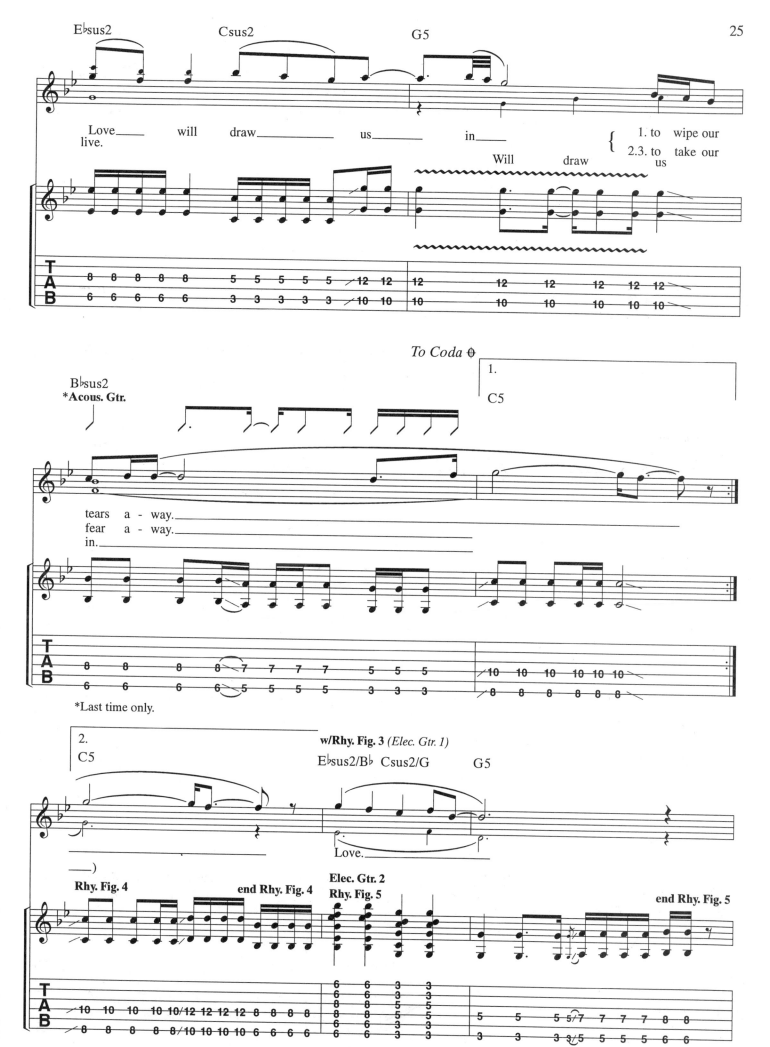

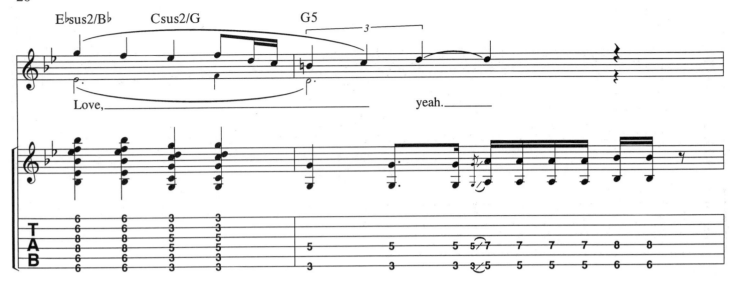

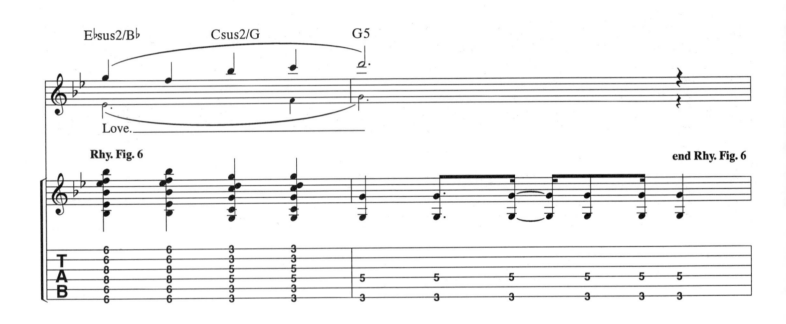

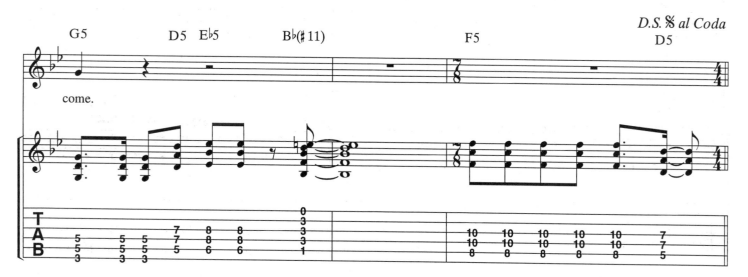

28

RUN TO THE WATER

All gtrs. tune down 1/2 step:

⑥ = E♭ ③ = G♭
⑤ = A♭ ② = B♭
④ = D♭ ① = E♭

Words and Music by
Edward Kowalczyk and Patrick Dahlheimer

*Two gtrs. arr. for one.

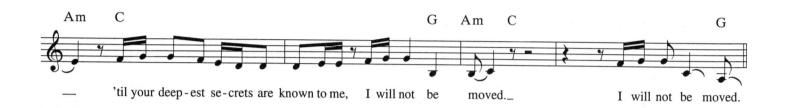

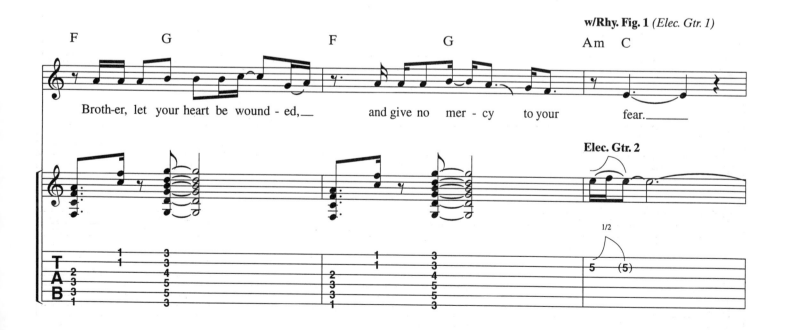

Run to the Water - 8 - 2
PG9911

34

*w/harmonizer effect set one octave higher.

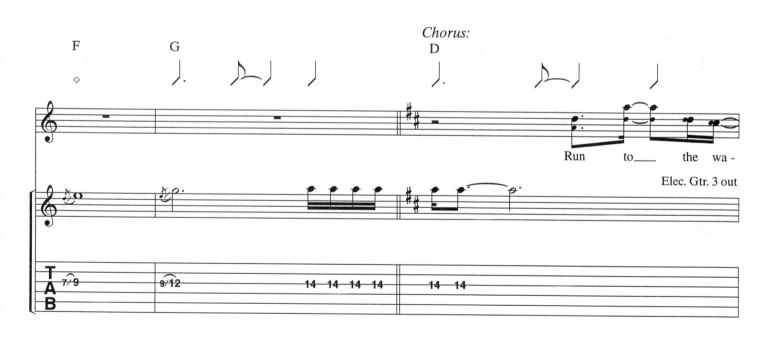

bro - ken.___ We'll cut through___ the mad - ness___ of these streets be - low___

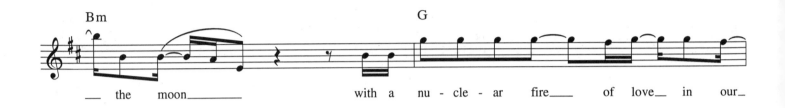

___ the moon_____ with a nu - cle - ar fire___ of love___ in our___

___ hearts. Rest eas - y, ba - by,___ rest eas - y and

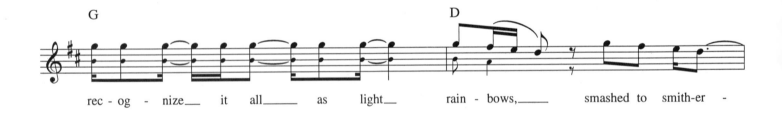

rec - og - nize___ it all___ as light___ rain - bows,___ smashed to smith - er -

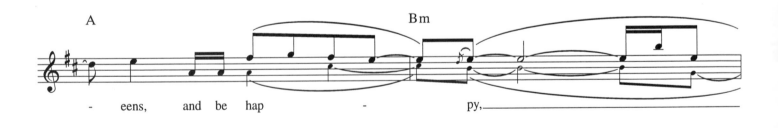

- eens, and be hap - py,_____

___ yeah._____ Run to___ the wa - ter___ and find_____

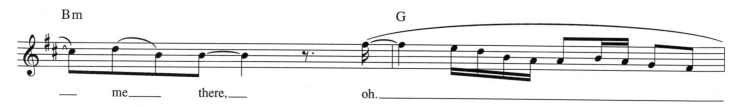

Bm   G

— me____ there,___   oh._____

w/Vocal Fill 1

D   A   Bm   G

— Run to__ the wa - ter,_____ yeah.____

Freely

D

Elec. Gtr. 1

Vocal Fill 1

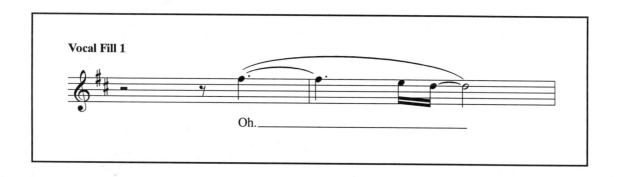

Oh._____

SUN

Words and Music by
Edward Kowalczyk

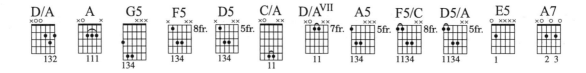

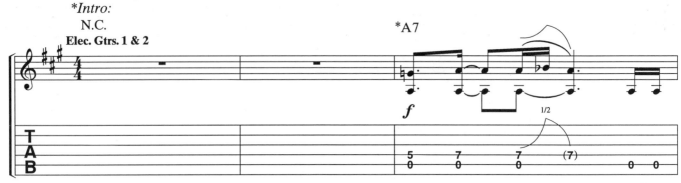

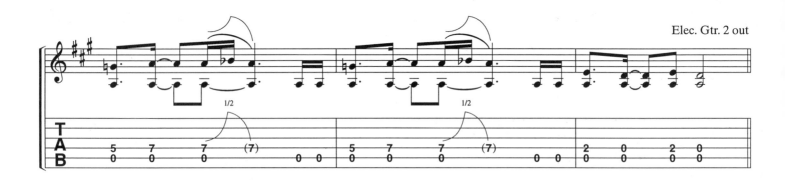

Sun - 8 - 1
PG9911

Let it run it's own game.___ Let it dance with it - self.

end Rhy. Fig. 1

I did-n't put it here,___ gon-na let it ride.

Elec. Gtr. 1

Rhy. Fig. 2

P.M.

Elec. Gtr. 2

Rhy. Fig. 2A

Got-ta mas - ter, cra - zy on the oth - er

end Rhy. Fig. 2

Cont. in slashes

end Rhy. Fig. 2A

Cont. in slashes

Elec. Gtrs. 1 & 2

D/A   A   D/A   A   D/A   A

side,_____   wak-in' me up.

Verses 2 & 3:
w/Rhy. Fig. 1 *(Elec. Gtr. 1)*

D/A   A   Elec. Gtr. 2 out   A7

2. I ain't got no   brains,___   I can't trust my   eyes.
3. Let the world be   the world.   Let the girl   be the girl.
(Spoken:) (Let the world be the world.   Let the

What good's a beau-ti - ful   day___   if you can't   see   the light?___
Let   her beau-ty   move ya.   Let her   dance   be your guide.
girl   be the girl.   Let her move   ya.   We gon - na

I can't find my fate,
Let your hun- ger grow,
dance.
well, then I must be blind___
but don't eat the fruit "too low."___
Groove.   *Too low.*

— with the force and fire of love___ that's tak- in' o- ver my mind,_
— Keep climb- in' for the kiss- es on the o- ther
Backing vocals tacet first time only.

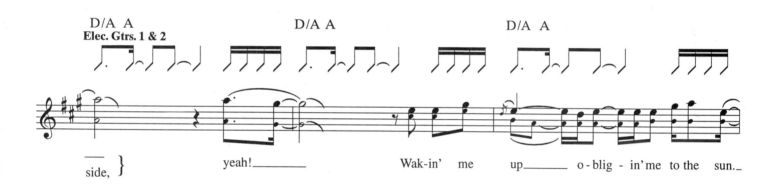

D/A A   D/A A   D/A A
Elec. Gtrs. 1 & 2
side, }   yeah!___   Wak- in' me up___ o- blig- in' me to the sun._

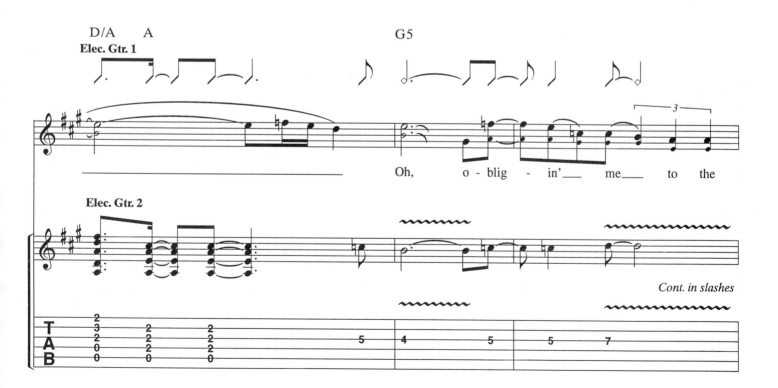

D/A A   G5
Elec. Gtr. 1
Oh, o- blig- in'___ me___ to the
Elec. Gtr. 2
Cont. in slashes

Sun - 8 - 4
PG9911

42

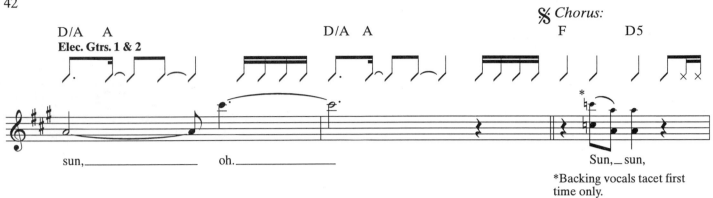

*Backing vocals tacet first
time only.

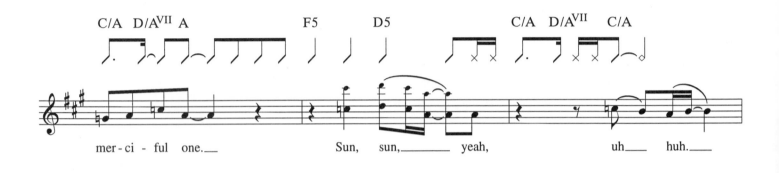

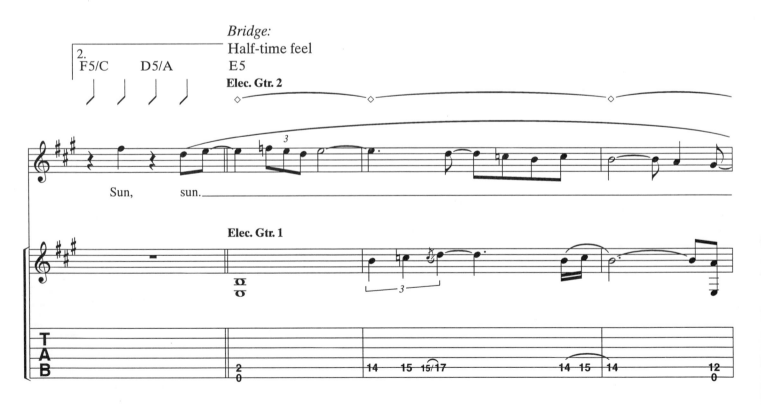

Sun - 8 - 5
PG9911

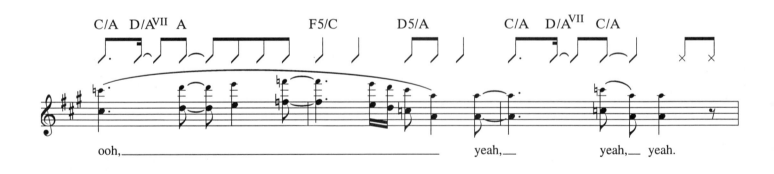

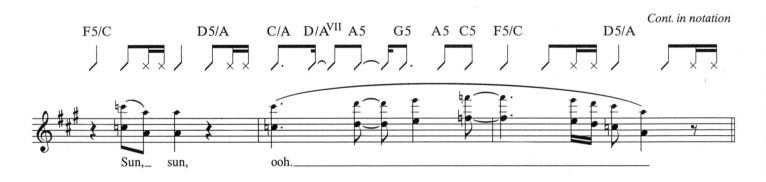

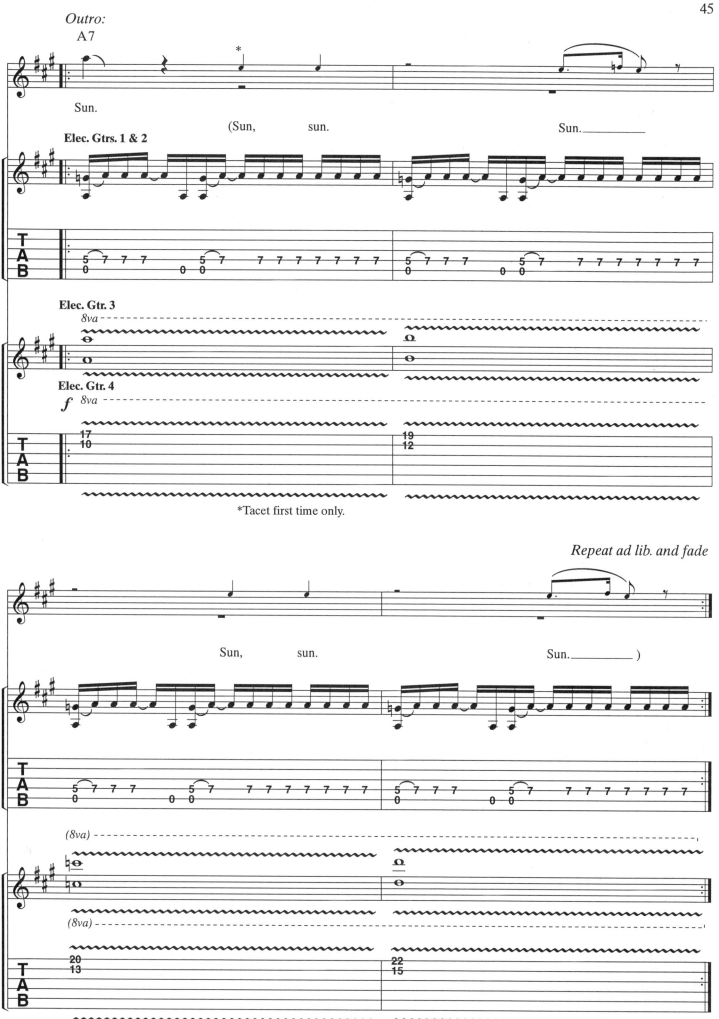

*Tacet first time only.

Repeat ad lib. and fade

VOODOO LADY

Words and Music by
Edward Kowalczyk and Chad Taylor

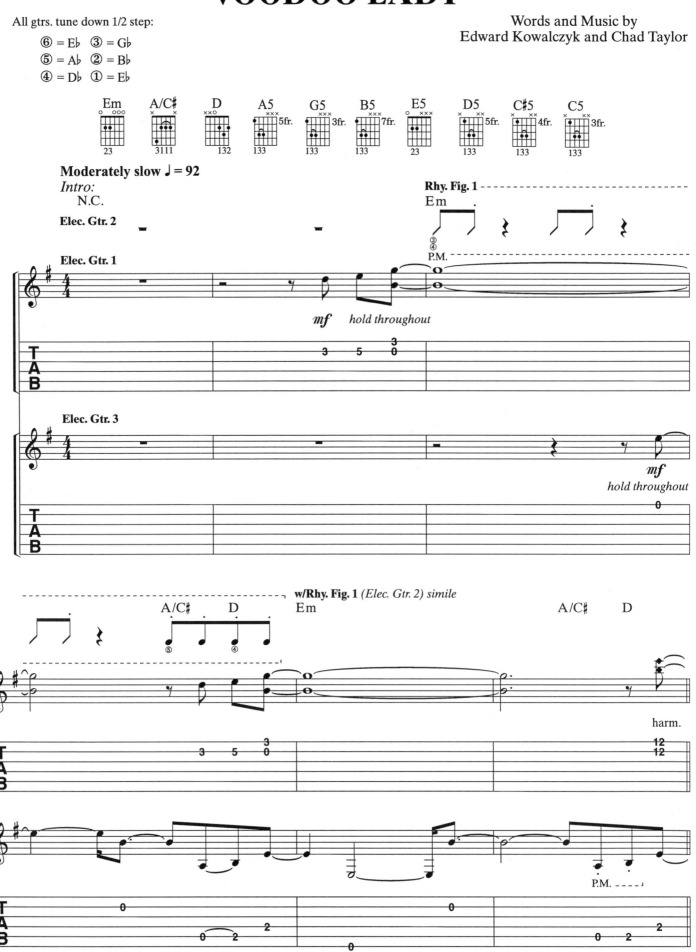

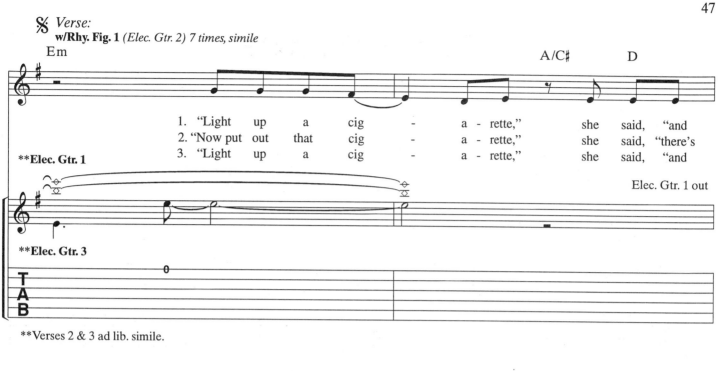

% *Verse:*
w/Rhy. Fig. 1 *(Elec. Gtr. 2) 7 times, simile*

Em   A/C♯   D

1. "Light up a cig - a - rette," she said, "and
2. "Now put out that cig - a - rette," she said, "there's
3. "Light up a cig - a - rette," she said, "and

Elec. Gtr. 1

Elec. Gtr. 1 out

Elec. Gtr. 3

**Verses 2 & 3 ad lib. simile.

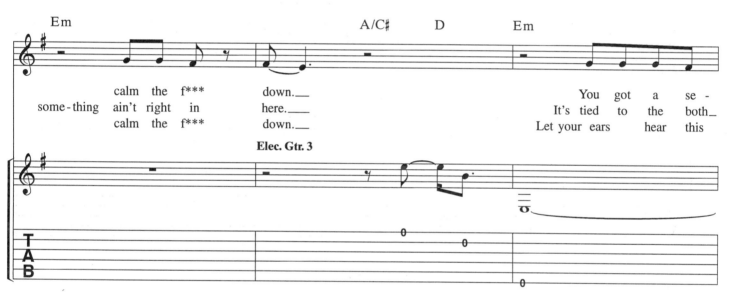

Em   A/C♯   D   Em

calm the f*** down.___   You got a se -
some-thing ain't right in here.___   It's tied to the both_
calm the f*** down.___   Let your ears hear this

Elec. Gtr. 3

A/C♯   D   Em   *To Coda II* ⊕

ri - ous side____ to you___ that could give the whole world a frown.___
___ of us.____ I ain't sure now; it is - n't clear.___
beau - ti - ful song____ that's hid - ing un - der - neath the sound."_

Voodoo Lady - 8 - 2
PG9911

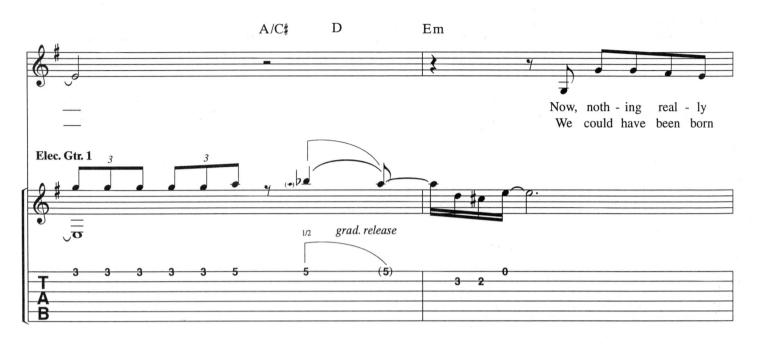

A/C♯   D   Em

Elec. Gtr. 1

Now, noth - ing real - ly
We could have been born

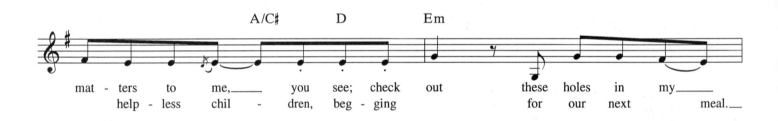

A/C♯   D   Em

mat - ters to me,____ you see; check out these holes in my____
help - less chil - dren, beg - ging for our next meal.__

A/C♯   D   Em   A/C♯ D

gown._____
Let your eyes lose their fo - cus a lit - tle, let your
I could be a voo - doo la - dy, just a

Elec. Gtr. 1

w/delay

Elec. Gtr. 3

50

Voodoo Lady - 8 - 5
PG9911

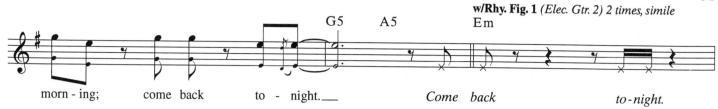

Voodoo Lady - 8 - 6
PG9911

Voodoo Lady - 8 - 8
PG9911

WHERE FISHES GO

Words and Music by
Edward Kowalczyk and Chad Taylor

All gtrs. tuned to "drop D" down a 1/2 step:

⑥ = Db   ③ = Gb
⑤ = Ab   ② = Bb
④ = Db   ① = Eb

D5   F   C(9)   Bb   C5   F5   G5   Db7(b5)   F6   Gsus2

Slowly ♩ = 78

Intro:
Fade in

F6 Gsus2

Riff 1

D5   F   D5   F

*Elec. Gtr. 1

mf

1/2   1/2

Backwards tape playback throughout section.

Verse:
w/Riff 1 *(Elec. Gtr. 1) 4 times, simile*

D5   F   D5   F   D5   F

1. Yeah,_ I found God_ and he was
ing now?_

**Elec. Gtr. 3

**Elec. Gtr. 2

ff Rhy. Fig. 1

1/2   1/2

**Verse 2 only.*

D5   F   D5   F   D5   F

ab - so - lute - ly noth - ing   like_____ me.
What's your plan?_____

mf

w/vol. swell 1/2

Elec. Gtr. 2 out
end Rhy. Fig. 1

He showed me up like some dime____ store hook-er who was plain____ to see.____
Yeah, I found God and he was ab-so-lute-ly just like____ me____

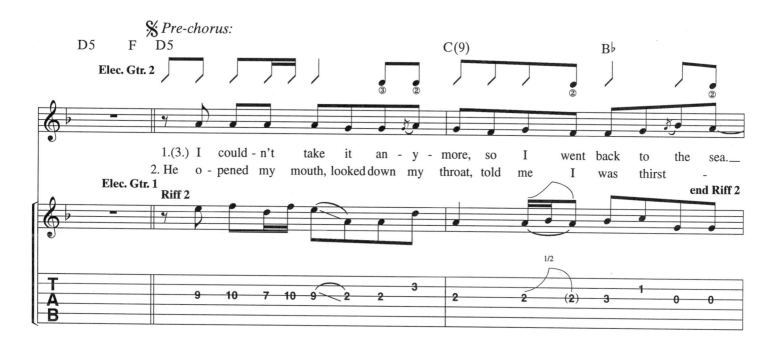

% Pre-chorus:

Elec. Gtr. 2

1.(3.) I could-n't take it an-y-more, so I went back to the sea.__
2. He o-pened my mouth, looked down my throat, told me I was thirst -

Elec. Gtr. 1
Riff 2 · end Riff 2

w/Riff 2 (Elec. Gtr. 1) 3 times, simile
Cont. rhy. simile

____ 'Cause__ that's where fish-es go__ when
y I been__ in this wa-ter all__ my

fish-es get the sense to flee.____
life, nev-er took the time to breathe, breathe,

1.
2. Where__ you go -

56

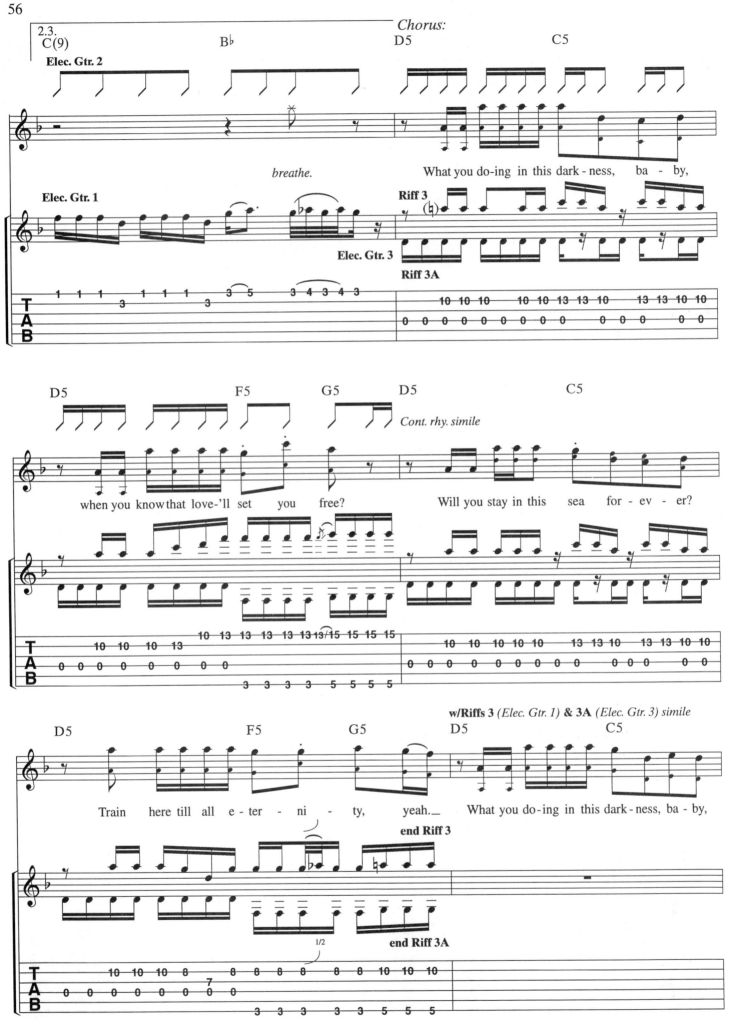

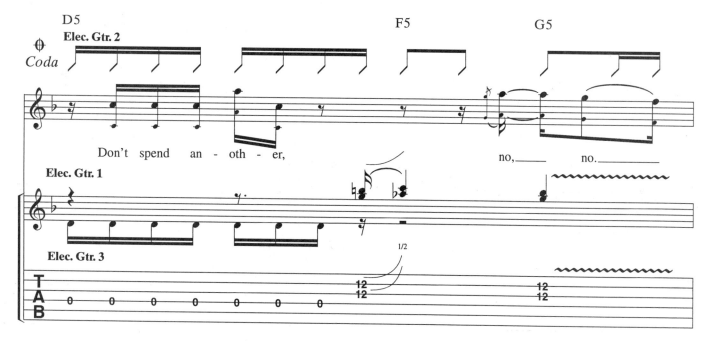

58

w/Riffs 3 *(Elec. Gtr. 1)* **& 3A** *(Elec. Gtr. 3) simile*

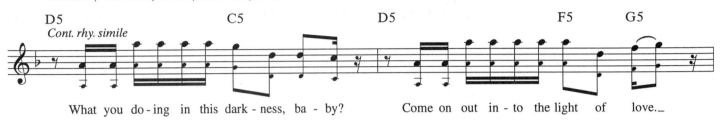

What you do-ing in this dark - ness, ba - by? Come on out in - to the light of love._

Come on out in - to the light of love, child._ Don't spend an - oth - er day_ liv - ing in the_

Outro:
w/Riff 1 *(Elec. Gtr. 1) 3 times, simile*
w/Rhy. Fig. 1 *(Elec. Gtr. 2)*

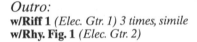

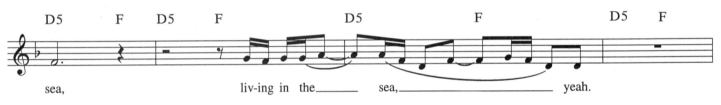

sea, liv-ing in the_____ sea,_____ yeah.

Fade

Yeah, I___ found God and he__ was_ ab - so-lute-ly__ noth-ing, but some-how_ just like me.

Elec. Gtr. 3

hold throughout section

Where Fishes Go - 5 - 5
PG9911

FACE AND GHOST
(The Children's Song)

Words and Music by
Edward Kowalczyk

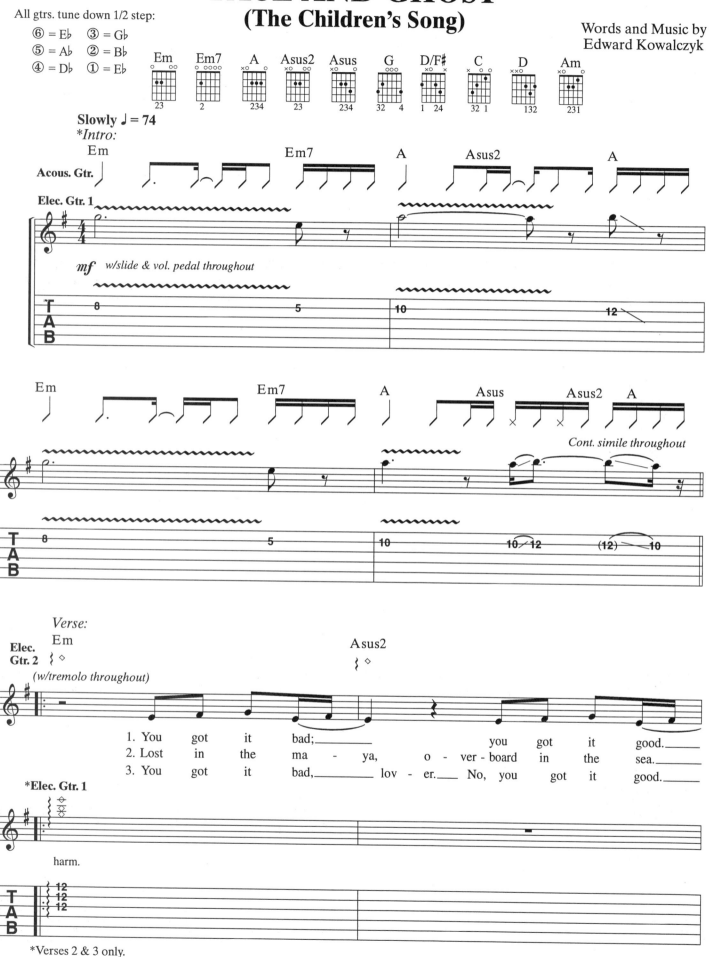

All gtrs. tune down 1/2 step:

⑥ = E♭ ③ = G♭
⑤ = A♭ ② = B♭
④ = D♭ ① = E♭

Em Em7 A Asus2 Asus G D/F# C D Am

Slowly ♩ = 74
*Intro:

*Verses 2 & 3 only.

1. You got it bad;_____ you got it good._____
2. Lost in the ma - ya, o - ver - board in the sea._____
3. You got it bad,_____ lov - er._____ No, you got it good._____

Face and Ghost - 5 - 1
PG9911

61

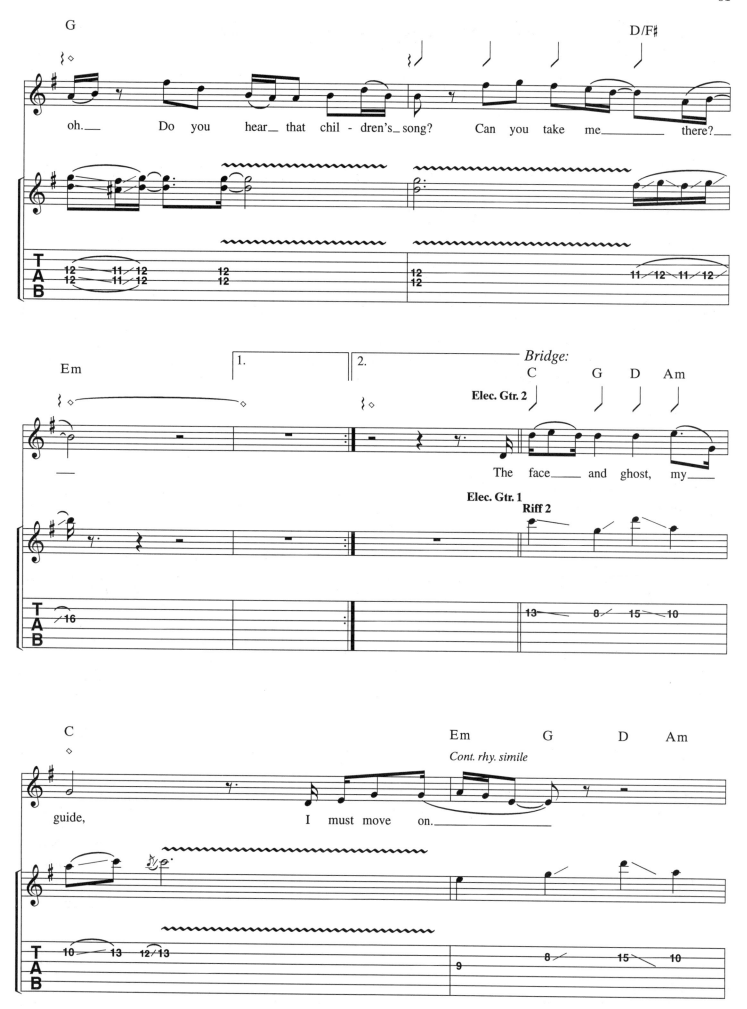

Face and Ghost - 5 - 3
PG9911

62

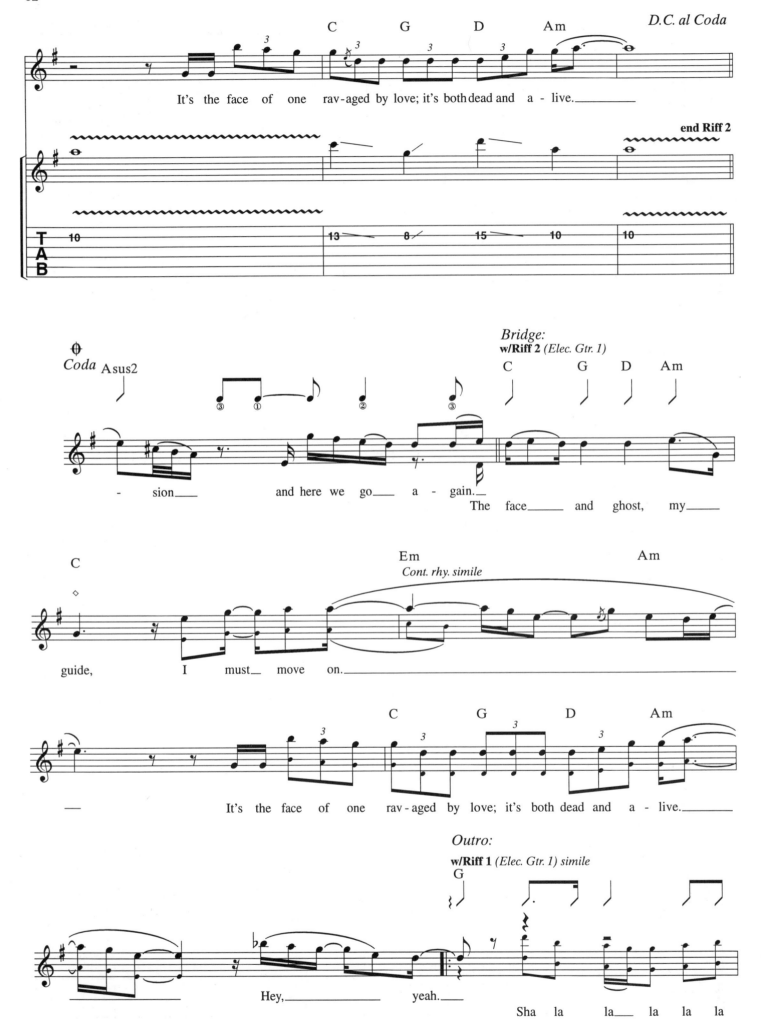

63

Face and Ghost - 5 - 5
PG9911

FEEL THE QUIET RIVER RAGE

Feel the Quiet River Rage - 8 - 1
PG9911

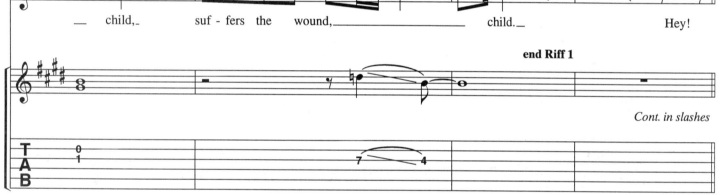

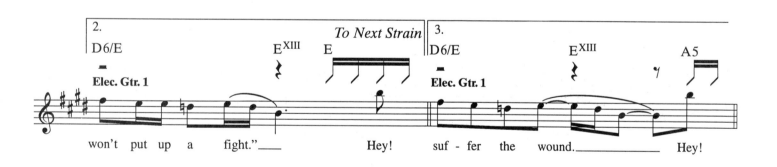

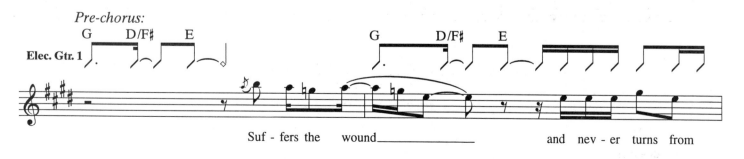

66

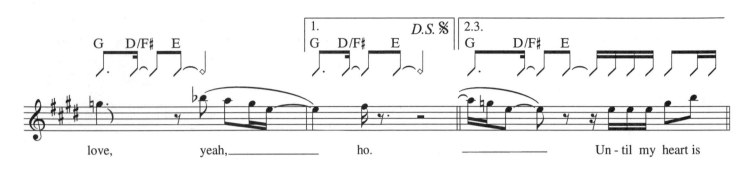

love, yeah, ho. Un-til my heart is

Chorus:

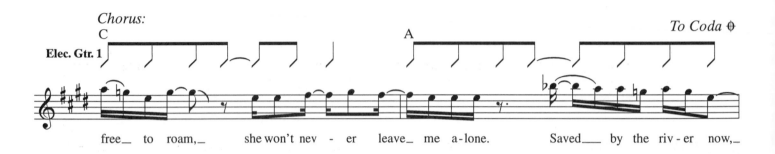

free to roam, she won't nev - er leave me a-lone. Saved by the riv-er now,

saved, yeah, yeah, yeah.

Interlude:

Coda

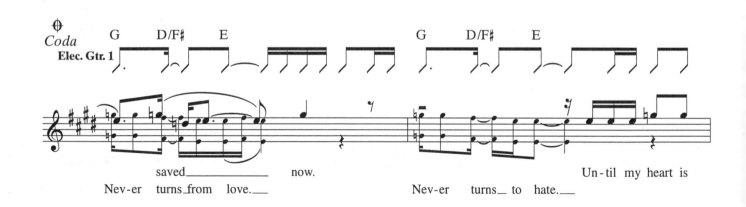

saved now. now. Un-til my heart is

Nev-er turns from love. Nev-er turns to hate.

Feel the Quiet River Rage - 8 - 3
PG9911

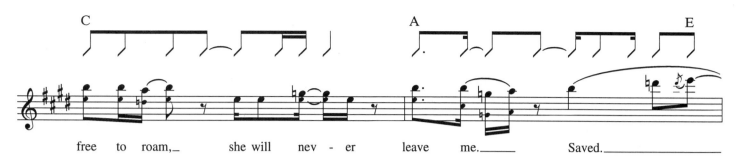

free to roam,___ she will nev - er leave me.___ Saved._____

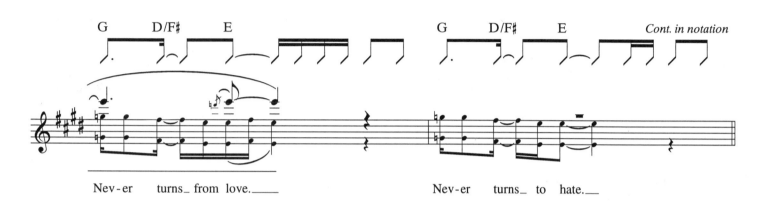

Nev - er turns_ from love.____ Nev - er turns_ to hate.__

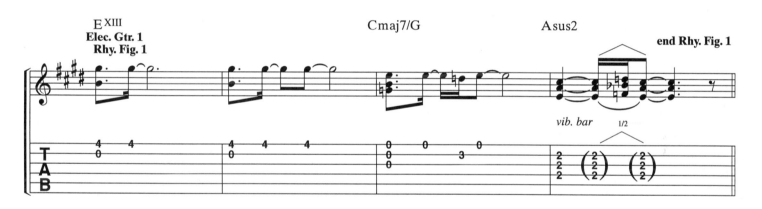

Al - ways suf - fers the wound,_____ nev - er turns__ from love,_

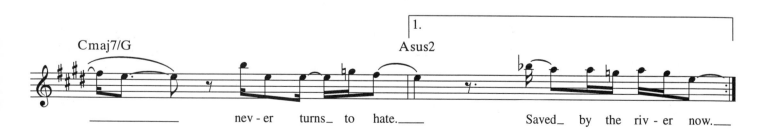

_____ nev - er turns_ to hate.___ Saved_ by the riv - er now.__

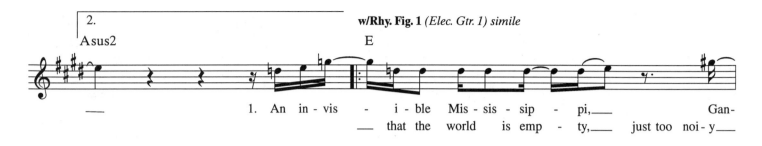

1. An in - vis - i - ble Mis - sis - sip - pi,___ Gan-
___ that the world is emp - ty,___ just too noi - y

- ges, or a Nile,_____ I can feel__ the qui - et riv - er rage,___ forc - in' my lips_
___ to hear the sound._____ I can feel__ the qui - et riv - er rage_____ and I'm fall-

___ in - to a___ smile.___ 2. Don't be - lieve_ - in' down,_ saved__ by the riv - er now,_

yeah,_____ yeah._ Oh._
Saved__ by the riv - er now. Saved__ by the riv - er now.

Elec. Gtr. 1

69

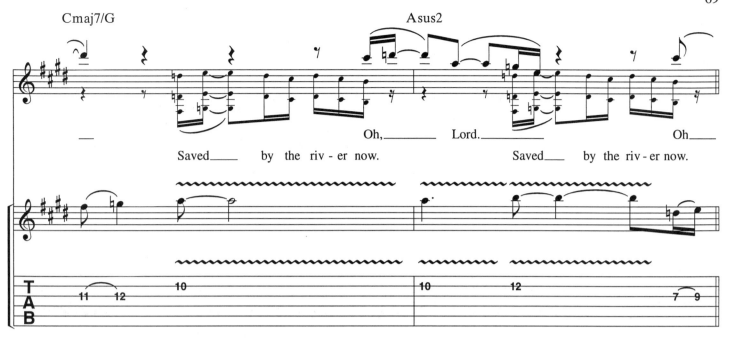

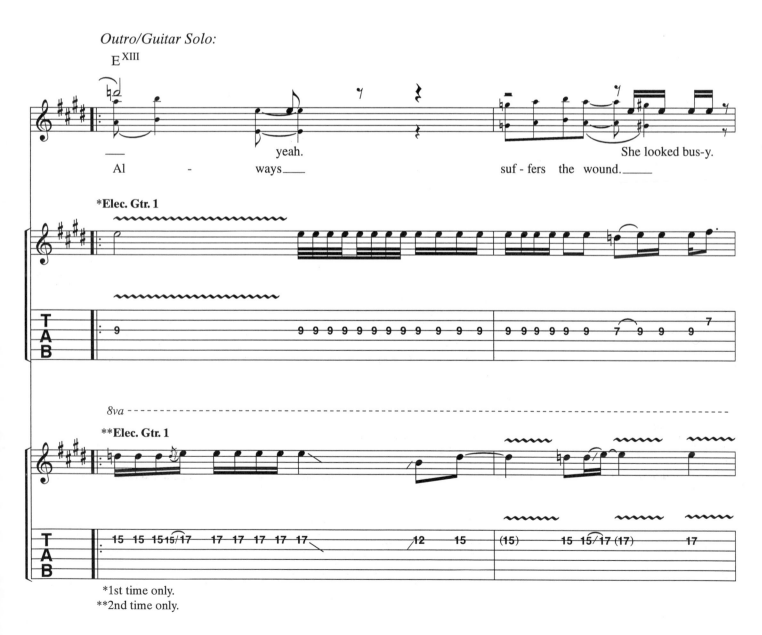

*1st time only.
**2nd time only.

Feel the Quiet River Rage - 8 - 6
PG9911

70

Feel the Quiet River Rage - 8 - 7
PG9911

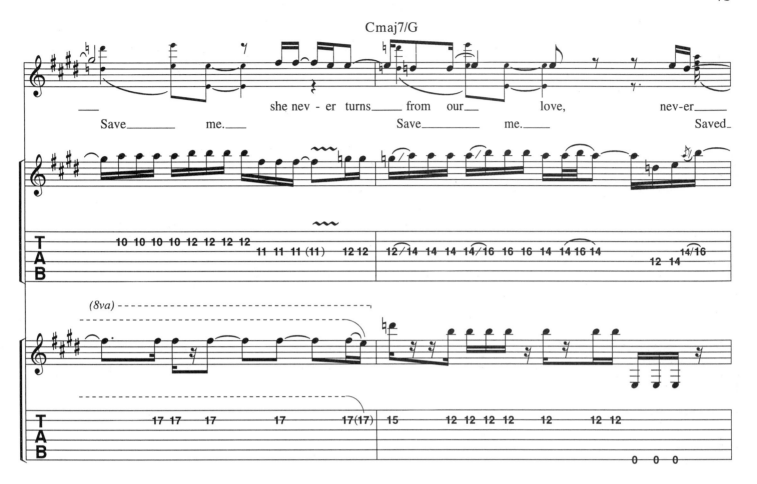

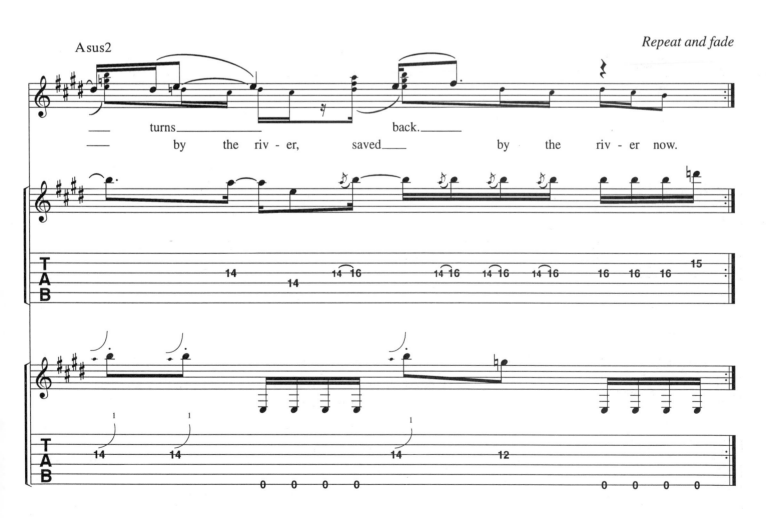

MELTDOWN

Words and Music by
Edward Kowalczyk

All gtrs. tune down 1/2 step:

⑥ = E♭   ③ = G♭
⑤ = A♭   ② = B♭
④ = D♭   ① = E♭

Moderate rock ♩ = 96

Intro:

74

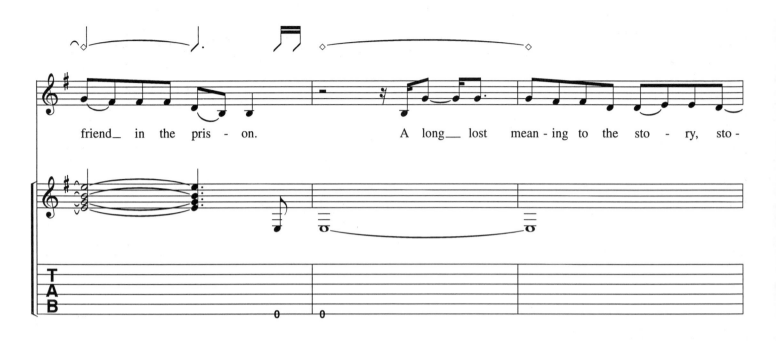

friend_ in the pris - on. A long_ lost mean - ing to the sto - ry, sto-

w/Rhy. Fig. 1 *(Gtr. 1) 2 times*
Em

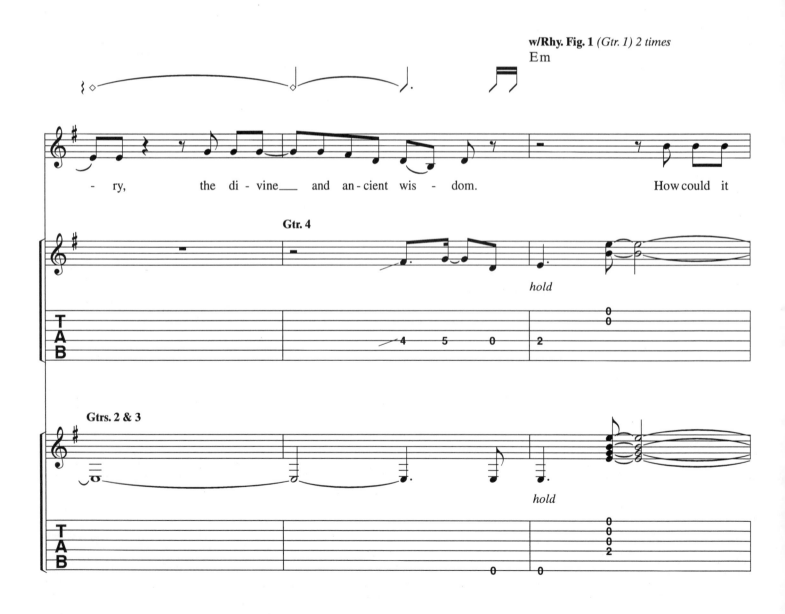

- ry, the di - vine_ and an - cient wis - dom. How could it

Gtr. 4

hold

Gtrs. 2 & 3

hold

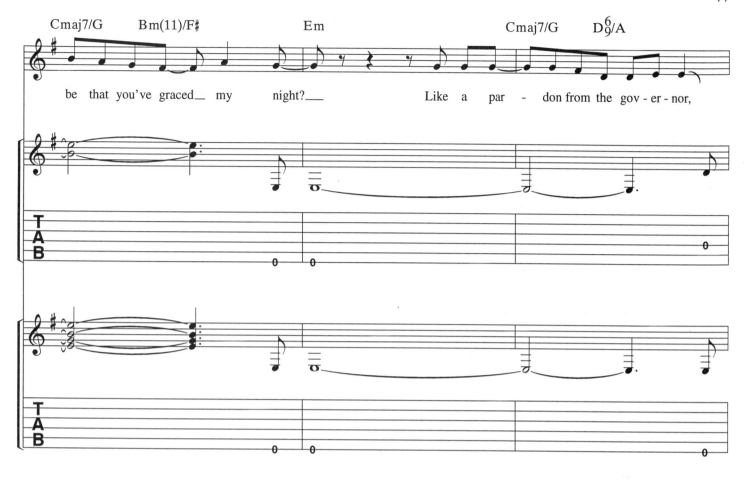

be that you've graced— my night?— Like a par - don from the gov - er - nor,

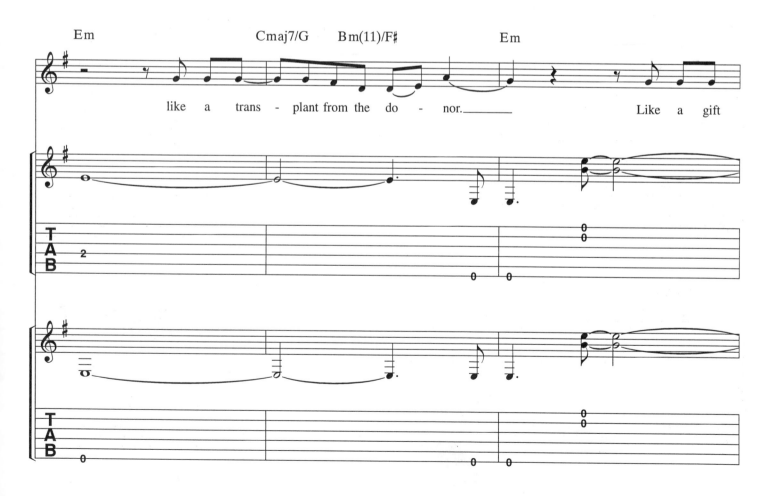

like a trans - plant from the do - nor._____ Like a gift

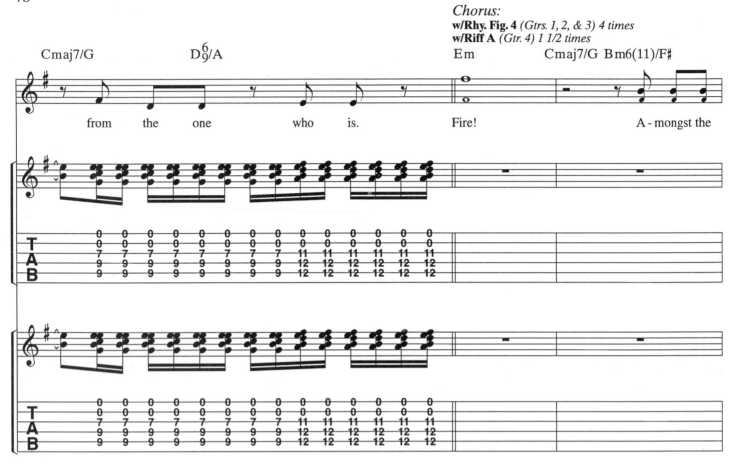

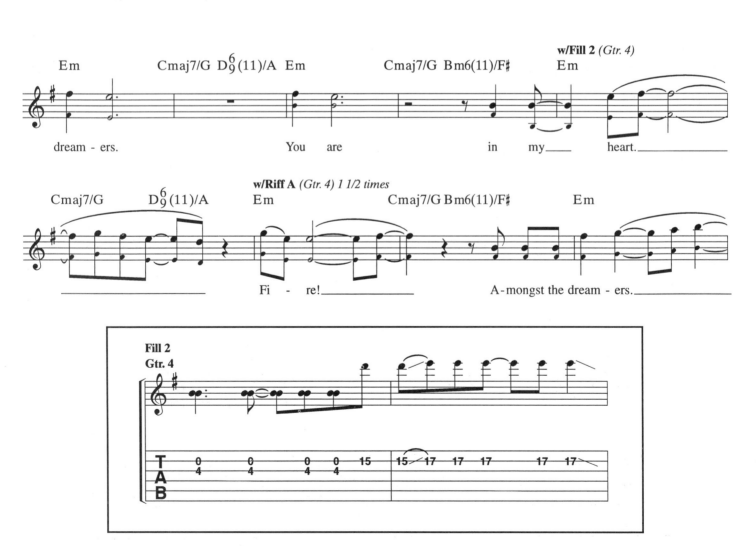

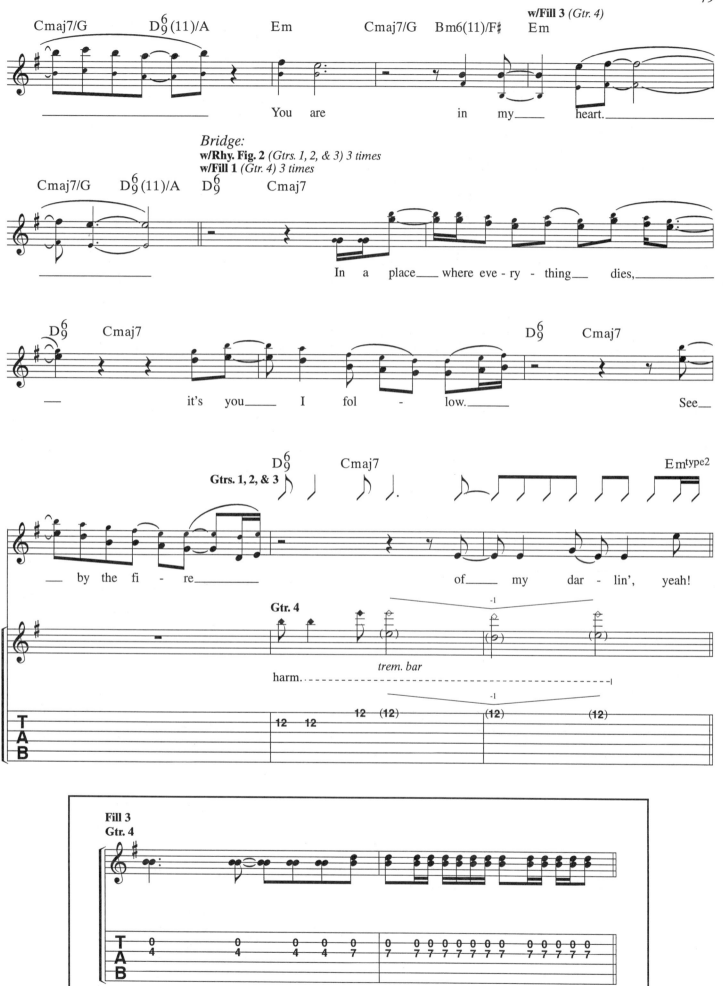

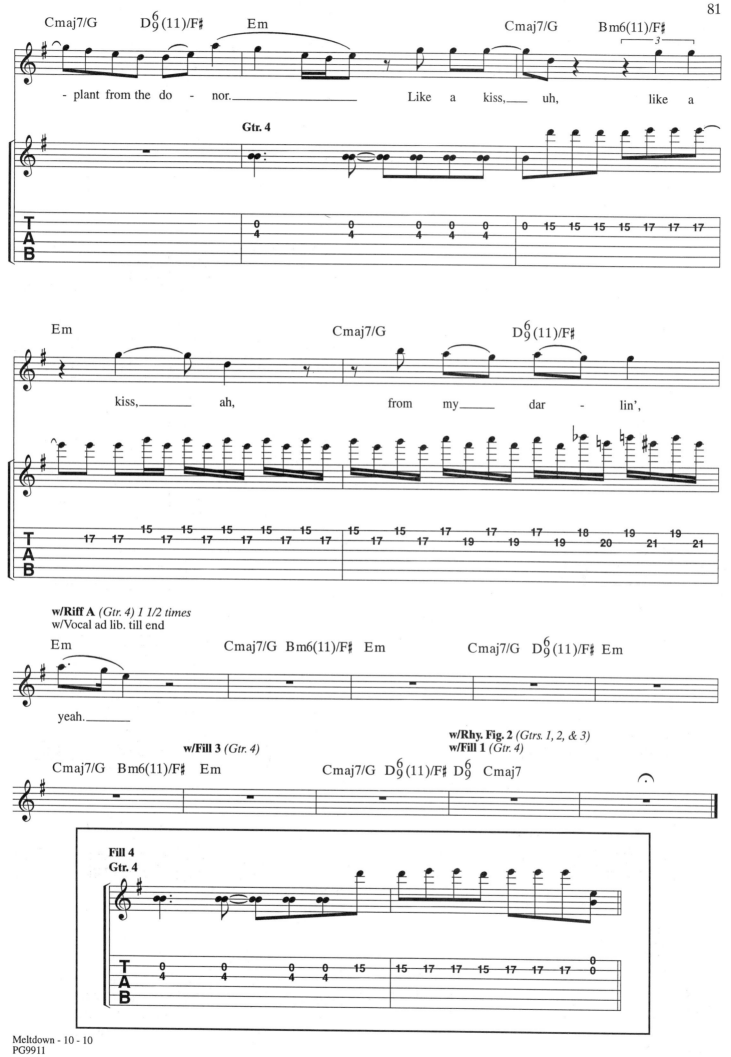

THEY STOOD UP FOR LOVE

Words and Music by
Edward Kowalczyk, Chad Taylor and Patrick Dahlheimer

All gtrs. tune down 1/2 step:

⑥ = E♭ ③ = G♭

⑤ = A♭ ② = B♭

④ = D♭ ① = E♭

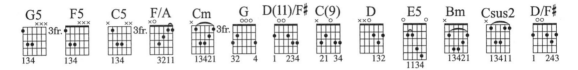

Moderately slow ♩ = 94

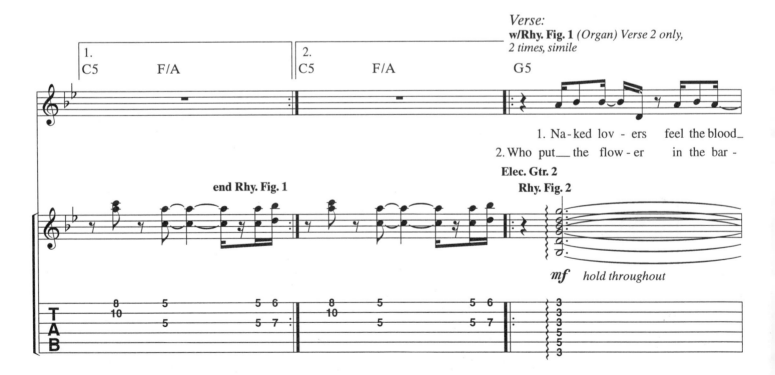

They Stood Up for Love - 8 - 1
PG9911

84

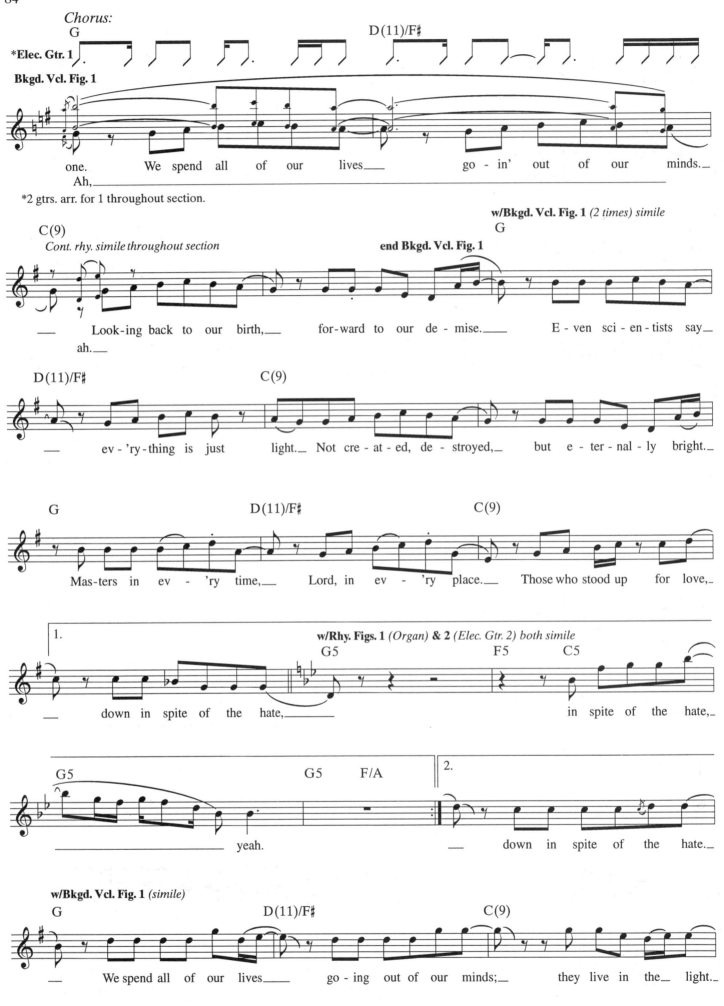

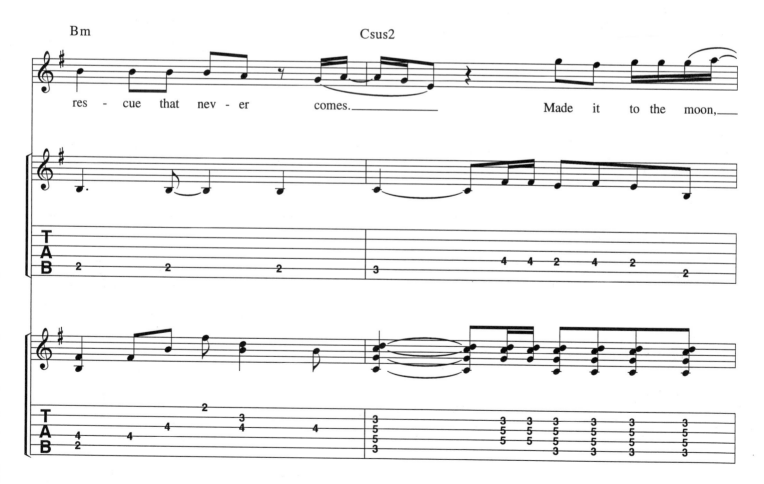

but we can't make it home._____ May - be

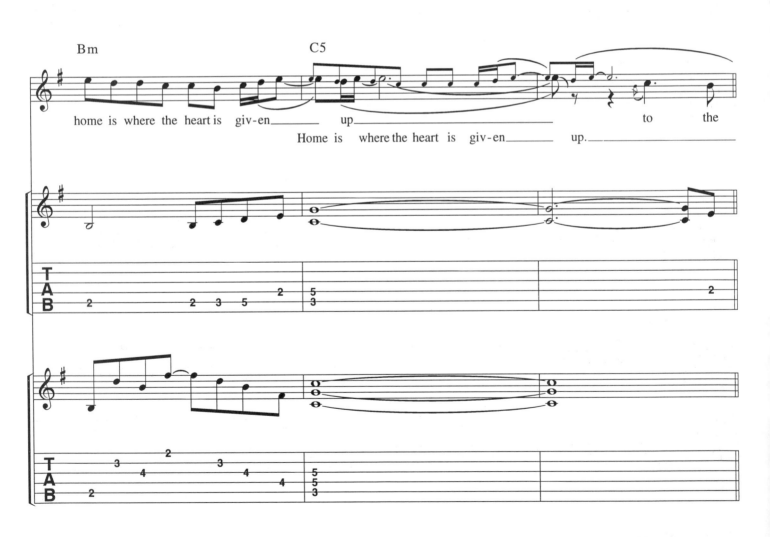

home is where the heart is giv-en_____ up_____

Home is where the heart is giv-en_____ up._____ to the

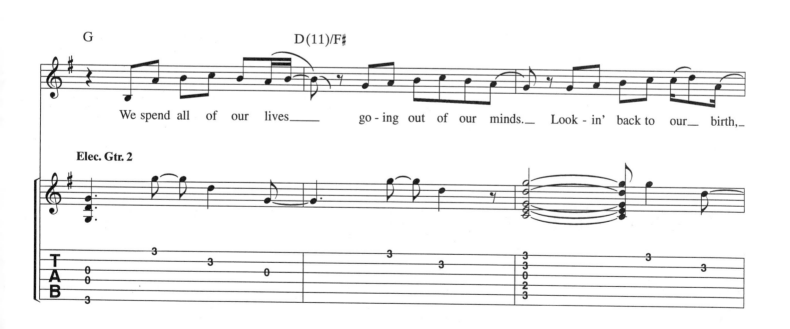

for - ward to our de - mise.
Ah.

We spend all of our___ lives___

P.M.

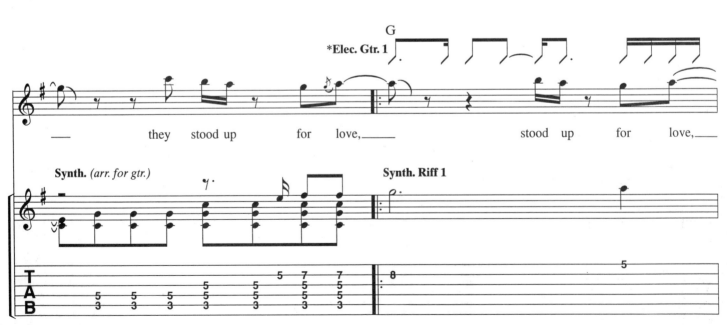

go - ing out of our minds.___ They live, they,___

*Elec. Gtr. 1

they stood up for love,___ stood up for love,___

Synth. (arr. for gtr.)

Synth. Riff 1

*2 gtrs. arr. for 1 to end.

stood up for love,_____ yeah,_____ yeah.____

They stood up for love,_____ yeah.____

Outro:

w/Bkgd. Vcl. Fig. 1 & Riff 1 *(Synth.) both simile*

Repeat and fade

We spend all of our lives_ go-ing out of our minds.____

Mas-ters in ev-'ry time._

Lead vcl. ad lib. on repeats.

WE WALK IN THE DREAM

Words and Music by
Edward Kowalczyk

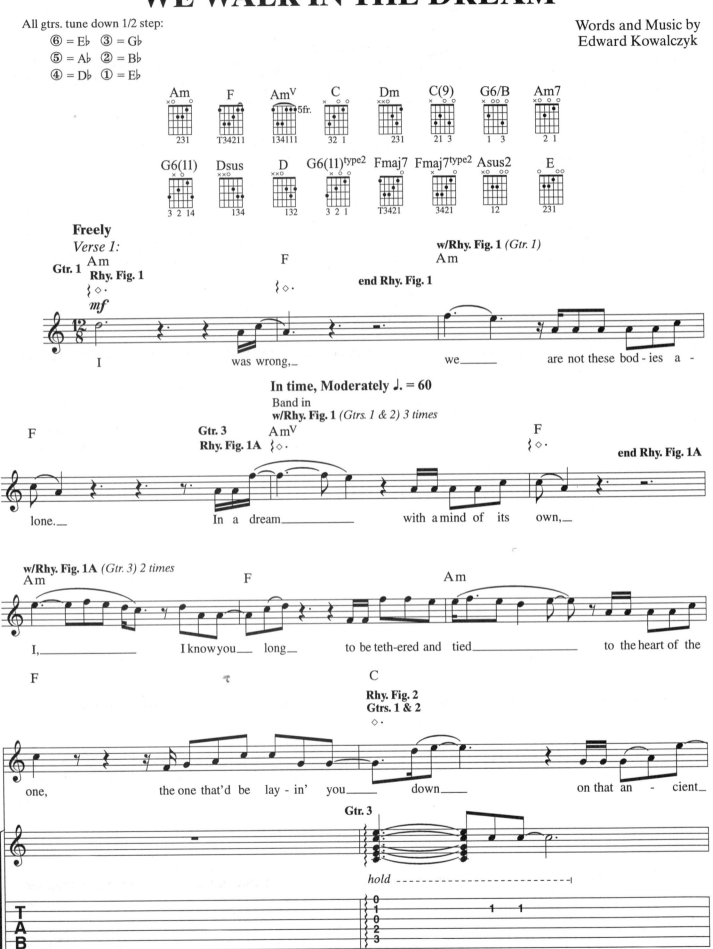

*Three gtrs. arr. for one.

own. Like an ea - gle cuts through the air, no time for

D.S. 𝄋 al Coda I

fear. Faith in his wings takes him there. Now we walk in the

hold

Coda I

Oh yeah, to live a life in love

Gtr. 3

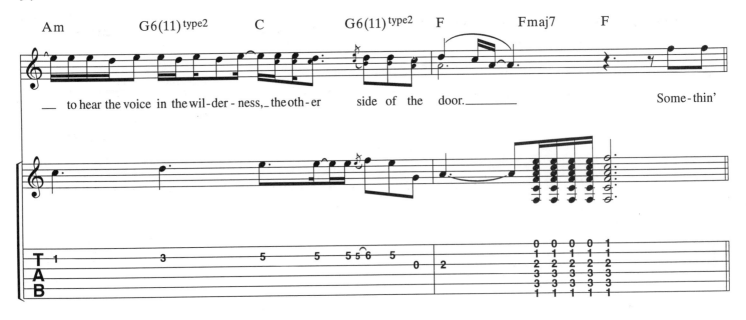

Am   G6(11)type2   C   G6(11)type2   F   Fmaj7   F

_ to hear the voice in the wil-der-ness,_ the oth-er   side of the   door._____   Some-thin'

Bridge:

Fmaj7type2

Gtr. 1
Rhy. Fig. 4

more!   More   than these

Gtr. 2
Rhy. Fig. 4A

hold

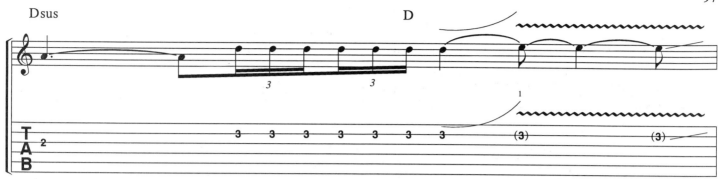

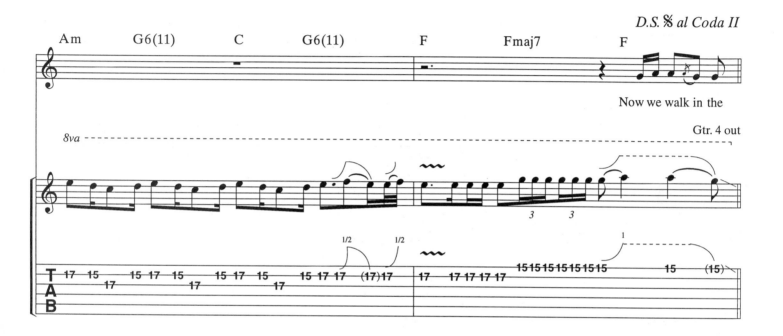

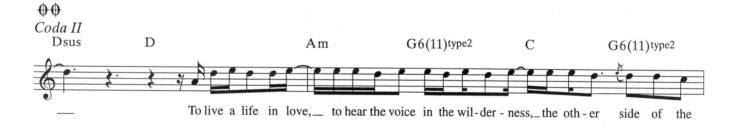

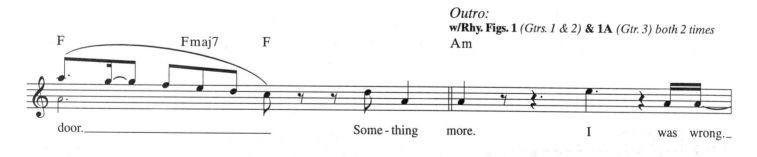

DANCE WITH YOU

Words and Music by
Edward Kowalczyk

All gtrs. tune down 1/2 step:

⑥ = E♭ ③ = G♭
⑤ = A♭ ② = B♭
④ = D♭ ① = E♭

D5 D5/C# Em G5 D A D/F# G5/F#

Slowly ♩ = 70
Intro:
D5   D5/C#

Gtr. 1 Rhy. Fig. 1

mf hold

Verse 1:
w/Rhy. Fig. 1 *(Gtr. 1) 3 times*

Em   G5   D5

Sit-tin' on__ the beach,

end Rhy. Fig. 1

Gtr. 2
Fill 1
8va -

mf *

*Vol. swells.

D5/C#   Em   G5

the is-land king of love,__ deep in Fi-ji-an seas,__ deep in some bliss-ful dream,

end Fill 1

fdbk.

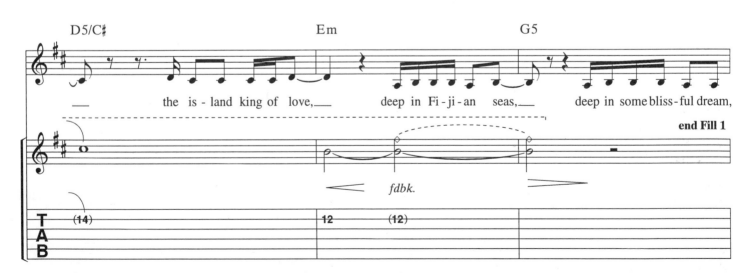

Dance With You - 7 - 1
PG9911

102

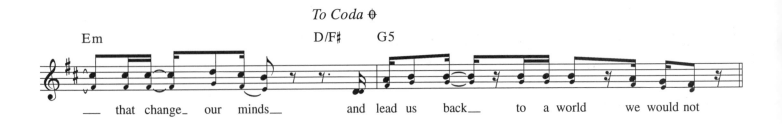

Dance With You - 7 - 5
PG9911

so much pain and rage. You know we got to find a way to let it go.

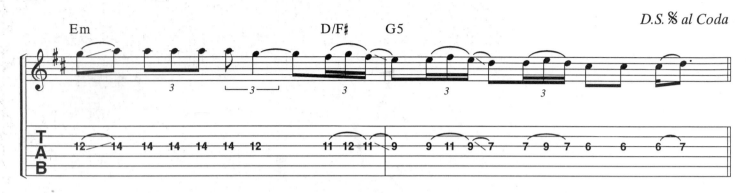

Outro:
w/Rhy. Figs 1 *(Gtr. 1)* **& 1A** *(Gtr. 3)* both 1 3/4 times
w/Fill 2 *(Gtr. 2)* **& Fill 4** *(Gtr. 4)* both 2 times

Coda

lead us back___ to a world we would_ not face,___ we would_ not face,

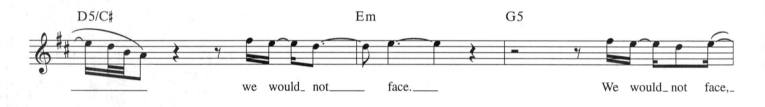

we would_ not_____ face.___ We would_ not face,_

we would_ not face,_____ we would_ not_____ face._____

Verse 3:
Sittin' on the beach,
The island king of love,
Deep in Fijian seas,
Deep in the heart of it all,
Where the goddess finally sleeps.
After eons of war and lifetimes
She's smilin' and free, nothin' left
But a cracking voice and a song, oh Lord.
(To Chorus:)